A TOMMY'S SKETCHBOOK

WRITINGS AND DRAWINGS FROM THE TRENCHES

LANCE-CORPORAL HENRY BUCKLE
EDITED BY DAVID READ
FOREWORD BY JACK RUSSELL MBE FRSA

First published 2012

The History Press
The Mill, Brimscombe Port
Stroud, Gloucestershire, GL5 2QG
www.thehistorypress.co.uk

British Library Cataloguing in Publication Data.
A catalogue record for this book is available from the British
Library.

ISBN 978 0 7524 6605 7

Typesetting and origination by The History Press
Printed in India

CONTENTS

No. 3 Tent, 'D' Company, 2nd Volunteer Battalion, The Gloucestershire Regiment. This photograph was taken at East Down Camp on Salisbury Plain in August 1900. Henry Buckle is believed to be the tall young man standing on the far right.

FOREWORD

I was thrilled to be asked to write the foreword to this book for a number of reasons. First and foremost, it is about a Gloucestershire man's record of his experiences in France in 1915. Henry Buckle was clearly a highly talented man, not only could he paint, he was observant as well as having a wry sense of humour. This and his indomitable spirit shines through despite the massive scale of human slaughter and suffering then encountered in the trenches.

Secondly, it reminds us of the huge contribution and sacrifice made by the men of Gloucestershire, mostly in The Gloucestershire Regiment. In those days the county was much larger than it is now and encompassed North Bristol, so their reach was wide. It should be remembered that The Gloucestershire Regiment sent over 40,000 men to the war and of those some 8,100 were killed, including my own great-uncle.

Thirdly, his talent as an artist is clear. While most of his pictures could be described as naïve, they are nonetheless beautifully composed and detailed.

They give us a much better idea of everyday life in the front line – the bath day picture with all the boots in line is a delight. His observations of some of the military characters are hilarious and I'm told hold true even today.

I thoroughly enjoyed the book and commend it to all those many thousands of families whose forebears went off to France to encounter the horror that was the Great War.

Jack Russell MBE FRSA
Gloucestershire, November 2011

INTRODUCTION

Henry Charles Buckle was a whitesmith from Tewkesbury. Before the outbreak of the Great War in August 1914, he had been a part-time soldier with 2nd Volunteer Battalion, The Gloucestershire Regiment since 1900. This became 5th (Territorial) Battalion in 1908. He volunteered for active service on 2 September 1914, giving his age as thirty years old, although in reality he was thirty-two, and knew it. Henry was married to Emily, and together they had a daughter, Alice Florence, who was aged five in 1914. A subsequent child died in infancy. His father, John, who died before the outbreak of the war, had been employed for many years as assistant verger of Tewkesbury Abbey Church, despite the fact that he was blind. Henry was invariably known to the family as 'Harry'. Emily, known as 'Dot', had grown up in a military family, her father, Company Sergeant-Major John Rollings having served twenty-one years in the Leinster Regiment.

Henry Buckle's period of service abroad was a relatively brief one. He went to France in March 1915, and was injured in October of that year when a trench collapsed on him, as a result of enemy shell-fire. The injury to his knee involved many months of treatment before he was pronounced unfit and discharged from the army in August 1916.

He kept a diary of his experiences which he typed up after he was invalided out of the army, omitting all the dates and many place names. He was a keen amateur photographer, and watercolourist, but it has to be said that his watercolours are by no means accomplished. However, together with his diary, Henry Buckle's paintings provide a fascinating insight into life in and out of the trenches in France and Belgium during 1915. Contemporary colour images from the front are all too rare, and Henry's charming and naïve pictures are full of exquisite details.

Despite Henry's enthusiasm for photography, no wartime photographs taken by him are known by us to have survived, although he did set up his own photographic studio in a farmhouse near Chelmsford, to take pictures of his chums. 1/5th Gloucesters were accompanied by a professional photographer from Cheltenham during their stay in Essex in 1914/15, and many of the pictures taken by him are held in the Soldiers of Gloucestershire Museum's collection. It might well be that one or more of them include images of Henry Buckle. We know what he looked like from post-war photographs, and his Army Medical Pension Record shows that he was tall for the time, over 5' 10", with dark brown hair and hazel eyes. The selection of photographs in the museum's collection that belonged to Henry Buckle date between 1900 and 1910, but they were probably not all taken by him. Some of them indeed might include Henry himself, but he does not say so in his own descriptions of them.

The flood of volunteers on the outbreak of the Great War led to many Territorial Battalions, including 5th Gloucesters, being split into two, later

'D' Company, 2nd Volunteer Battalion, The Gloucestershire Regiment. Tidworth Park Camp, Salisbury Plain in August 1903.

three, and brought up to strength. 1/5th Battalion, The Gloucestershire Regiment got the cream of the crop, while 2/5th tended to be composed of the younger and older men, as well as those who weren't quite fit enough. Perhaps Henry was permitted to lower his age in order to get him in to 1/5th Gloucesters. He was posted to 'B' Company.

1/5th Gloucesters left Swindon for Danbury (near Chelmsford) in August 1914 for a training period which lasted until March 1915. They formed part of 145th Brigade, 48th (South Midland) Division. Henry Buckle landed with the battalion at Boulogne on 29 March and in April they arrived at Steenvorde.

48th Division was assigned to the Ploegsteert ('Plugstreet') Wood sector under the command of III Corps, Second Army. On 28 June 1915, 1/5th Battalion was in billets at Allouagne as part of IV Corps Reserve, resting and training for the next couple of weeks. By late July 1915, 1/5th Gloucesters were moved forward once again to line the trenches opposite Serre. In late September 1915 they were entrenched in the front-line village of Hébuterne, alternating with stays in billets at the villages of Bus and Sailly, among others.

The front-line positions occupied by 48th Division were much engaged in sporadic fighting and patrol work over the next six or more months, Henry Buckle being injured during this period.

Henry Buckle's diary and album of paintings and drawings are held by the Soldiers of Gloucestershire Museum. His spelling and grammar are somewhat idiosyncratic, but have mostly been retained for the transcript in this book. His punctuation, however, has had to be radically altered,

"Jimmy"

The "5th" Glosters" Drill Hall at Tewkesbury

The "Miniature" Rifle Butts

The "Orderly Room" Side

Three "Old" Veterans

A page from one of Henry Buckle's albums showing 5th Gloucesters' Drill Hall at Tewkesbury, c.1910.

for he seemed to have little idea of when to use a full stop. The diary itself was certainly not updated daily, and it has not always been possible to reconcile some of the events and places described with those written up in the Battalion War Diary or other personal accounts written by soldiers serving with 1/5th Gloucesters. The most likely explanation for this is that Henry's movements did not always exactly match those of the battalion, and in his immediate world it was the movements and billets of his own platoon and company which were of most interest to him.

Most of Henry's pictures were annotated by Henry himself, with written notes on the paintings themselves, or on their reverse, or in the album; in many cases, all three. In these descriptions Henry often provided place names and dates, but again, his spelling of French and Belgian place names is often wayward, e.g. Gomercourt for Gommecourt. However, his spellings have largely been retained. Henry sent the paintings back to England from France and Belgium, usually in groups of four it seems. They may well have all gone to his wife, Emily, but where they are addressed it is to someone called 'Beck'. Henry and Emily's young daughter was called Alice, and although it is possible that 'Beck' might have been a nickname for either one of them, it is not known for sure. Most of the paintings are the size of a large postcard, and 'Beck' was advised to hold them at arm's length for viewing to obtain the best effect.

As Henry's paintings do not cover the period of his training in England in 1914 and 1915, and very few of them come from the time of his hospitalisation in 1915 and 1916, these two periods have therefore been partially illustrated instead with other photographs from the Soldiers of Gloucestershire Museum collection.

After the Great War, Henry settled with his wife and daughter in Harrogate and made a living as a freelance photographer. He sold photographs of Yorkshire news events to local and national newspapers, and also wrote a regular column for a motorcycle magazine. He is also known to have produced a collection of photographs of the fishing industry in Yorkshire in the 1930s, particularly around Whitby.

Henry Buckle died in Harrogate on 27 April 1954, aged seventy-two.

The Soldiers of Gloucestershire Museum is most grateful to his nephew, Brian Rollings, who donated the Henry Buckle Archive to the museum, and was able to help with some biographical details.

David Read
The Soldiers of Gloucestershire Museum,
November 2011

On the reverse of many of his paintings Henry wrote notes, often very detailed, describing the subject matter.

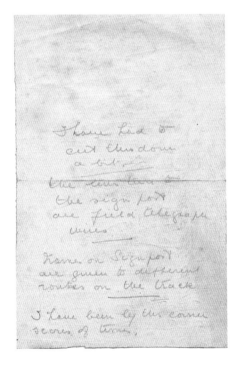

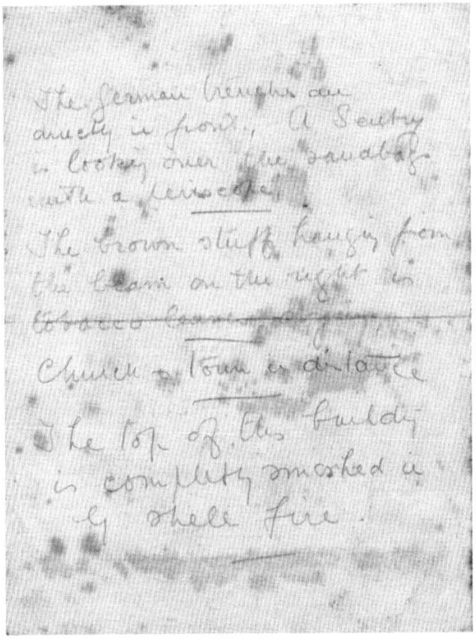

The German trenches are directly in front. A Sentry is looking over the sandbags with a periscope.

The brown stuff hanging from the beam on the right in ~~tobacco~~

Church & Town in distance

The top of this building is completely smashed up by Shell fire.

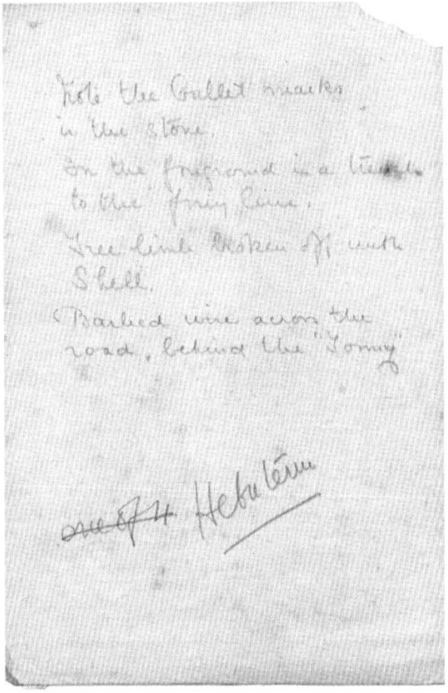

Note the bullet marks in the stone

In the foreground is a trench to the firing line

Tree limbs broken off with Shell

Barbed wire across the road, behind the 'Tommy'

Hebuterne

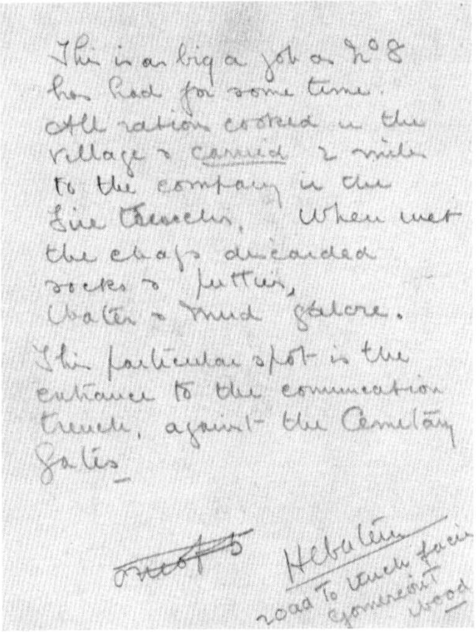

This is as big a job as No 8 has had for some time. All ration cooked in the village & ~~carried~~ 2 miles to the company in the fire trenches. When met the chaps discarded socks & putties, Water & mud galore.

This particular spot is the entrance to the communication trench, against the Cemetery Gates

Hebuterne
road to trench face
Gommecourt wood

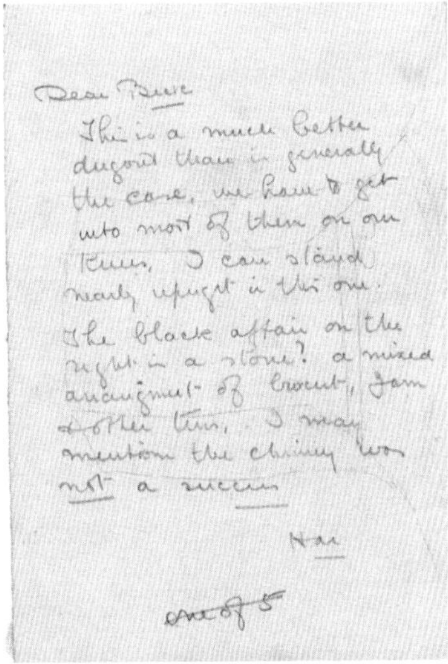

Dear Burt

This is a much better dugout than is generally the case, we have to get into most of them on our knees, I can stand nearly upright in this one. The black affair on the right is a stove? a mixed arrangement of biscuit, jam & other tins. I may mention the chimney was not a success

Hai

Harry and Dot on a motorcycle Jaunt in the 1920s.
Their daughter Alice took the photograph.

The First World War Diary of 2746 Lance-Corporal Henry Buckle

1/5th (Territorial) Battalion, The Gloucestershire Regiment

New recruits. 1/5th Battalion, The Gloucestershire Regiment. 2nd September, 1914. This photograph was taken on the very day Henry Buckle enlisted.

AUGUST/SEPTEMBER 1914

Henry Buckle was attested and embodied at Tewkesbury on 2 September 1914.

All the newspapers are appealing for men with any pretensions to military service to rejoin at once. It will be all over in about 8 months, or a year at most.

Wrote the Barracks at B___ *[Bristol]*, told them about my 5 years Signals and 10 years Territorial service. Barracks replied they are full up, so wrote the old depot in the Midlands, who replied, 'Come at once if fit.'

Went to the local doctor, who gave me the once over, shook hands and wished me good luck.

Made the necessary arrangements for leaving home for an indefinite period, took a toothbrush, a razor and a bag full of hope, and went.

Arrived at the depot; they wanted me to speak at a public meeting the same night.

Examined by the official M.O. *[Medical Officer]*; three of us passed fit in ten minutes.

Am billited in a public house, ten of us altogether, no uniforms, just a square of card with the name of the Regiment stamped on, together with a bit of red, white and blue ribbon attached, and such was sufficient to proclaim to the world at large, that we were members of the British Army.

Soldiers of 1/5th Battalion, The Gloucestershire Regiment at South Primrose Hill, Chelmsford. 1914.

Been five days in this billet now, parades in the square, bits of footwork and things, but generally killing time.

We now have free entry to Picture houses and the like, and lots of people come to watch us on the square at foot drill, etc., etc.

It has been rather surprising today to see the vast quantity of huge wagons and lorries which are passing through here on their way to the South Coast, an almost continuous stream bearing names from all over the north of England, and many places in Scotland.

We hear we are going to Chelmsford tomorrow, that is where the Regiment is at present. There is great excitement among the lads who have girls locally.

An awfull rowdy sendoff to Chelmsford yesterday. The local band blared our way to the station, cheers for everything and everybody, the war will be over in a few weeks. There was a goodly collection in our carriage, a Schoolmaster, a Commercial Traveller (soap I think), an engineer, two clerks, a millwright, a couple of labourers, and another old Terrier *[i.e., a pre-war Territorial soldier]* like myself, all young fellows full of the spirit of jubilant youth. Feel a wee bit ancient among this lot, but have visions of rapid promotion.

Absolute dissolutionment of promotion on arrival for nearly the first person to see was Sergt W___. Used to be awfully pally with him, but he just about cut me dead. 'You here!' was his only remark. Sergts ARE Sergts these days.

14 of us in a Marquee tent – very poor these tents. So cold, and it's too many together, although we are good pals; it's like the old camping days, but no fun now it's getting cold weather.

1/5th Battalion, The Gloucestershire Regiment on parade.
Chelmsford, 1914–1915. (right wing). This includes 'A' and 'B'
Companies. Henry Buckle was in 'B' Company.

What a farce, although a great many of us know foot and rifle drill backwards, we have been now a week on right and left turn, sickening.

No uniform yet, the old blue suit looks a mess, and boots are nearly done, three of our pals do not mess with us, (that is, squat in the field), they go down town to a restaurant; can't afford that.

Rumours of uniform this week, shall then look tidy perhaps – could do with boots as well.

Now moved into a billet, not before time. Dropped lucky into a nice place although it's only supposed to be for sleeping on a mattress on the floor. We have our meals here as well, bringing them from the field, which is only across the road. Nice people these, and we actually sit at a table again in the warmth of a room.

Obtained a pair of boots today, also a rifle (old pattern) [*The 1895 Pattern 'Long' Lee-Enfield rifle. Shortages of the later Short Magazine Lee-Enfield meant that many Territorial and New Army battalions were at first issued with obsolescent or 'stop-gap' equipment*]. The rifle seems familiar again, but the boots —! Oh lord, had job to manage the day out with them.

This afternoon we were served with uniform. Goodness what a fit, but don't shoot the tailor he's doing his best. It was take it or leave it, but parade in khaki tomorrow. Been busy tonight, taking tucks (or whatever they are) in and out, the landlady very helpful.

My giddy aunt, what a parade, the only thing was we were nearly all the same colour, misfits galore. At the dinner hour we had a general swop round with caps and tunics, resulting in a much more presentable appearance this afternoon, like a row of Turveydrops from Bleak House [*Mr Turveydrop is a character who runs a dance academy in Charles Dickens' novel* Bleak House. *Henry is comparing the newly kitted-out recruits with the smartly turned-out girl students of the academy 'Turveydrops'*].

What rumours today, millions of Russians passed through last night, France must be full and we are going to Egypt or somewhere hot, for there are trucks of pith helmets at the station! But cannot meet anyone who has actually seen either Russians or Helmets so far.

Made up into companies today, subdivided into platoons (new affair to me). Our Lieut. is a fellow from the old home town; also his brother is here as well. Jolly nice lads, knew their father very well, had a good chat about the old place.

Have been at bayonet practice nearly all day, you dash up and jab at a bag of straw; suppose the Germans will be doing likewise.

The local people have fixed up quite a good Soldiers Hall. Coffee and Buns at night at very reasonable charges, and most evenings there is a free concert. The staff is all voluntary, and we give a hand when required, it certainly is a place where one can spend an hour in congenial company, and I salute the promoters.

This day we have been fitted up with somebody's idea of what a Soldier should wear in battle with a modern foe. Save us, of all the donkey harness that ever was, this beats the Spaniards: a pair of huge leather pouches in front, very painfully secured with ponderous thick straps

Band of 1/5th Battalion, The Gloucestershire Regiment. c.1914.

sufficiently hefty to hold a bullock. We have been wrestling with this all day, we should be provided with a similar affair like the Zoo people use to saddle upon the elephants. What these things will be like with 50 to 60 rounds of ammunition in each and 20 miles to go. Ye Gods! *[Shortages of the modern 1908 Pattern webbing, which was made of closely woven, heavy-duty cotton, meant that a stop-gap soldier's harness made of leather was rushed into production in 1914. Although this 'donkey harness' was serviceable, it was less comfortable than the 1908 Pattern webbing, and Henry Buckle was not impressed.]*

Equipment parade today, these johnnies do not credit us with any horse sense. Detailed instructions on how to fasten a strap, the red tape is really astounding. In orders today we cannot go outside the billet without wearing a belt, even if one wears an overcoat, the belt must be underneath, (the M.P.s have orders to see to this). The sore point is, that to get this belt the equipment has to be taken all to pieces, to say nothing of putting it together again for the morrow. Usque ad nauseam.

The Sergt. idea is clean gone now. Did a guard last night and today, to see that the meat did not cut up rough with the cheese, or little things like that, also waggled my rifle at various Brass Hats. Turned out the guard as per orders, for the passing of the battalion although they were half a mile away … La la, M'sieur Chauvelin *[A reference to Citizen Chauvelin, the villain in* The Scarlet Pimpernel *by Baroness Orczy].*

Got my camera from home today. Mrs. B___ has kindly cleared a shelf in her pantry for me to develop on, hope to get a few pictures. Our big pots have whipped quite a good band together.

The aforesaid band made its debut today, and it will be jolly good on a long march, for we often do 15 or 20 miles. We also had our sports this afternoon — managed to get some good pictures, the camera is in great demand to take portraits of the boys for them to send home. Mrs. B's pantry is working overtime.

We have had a parade with a long speech from the C.O. [*Commanding Officer*] the outcome of which was asking us all to volunteer for service abroad and the majority of us immediately signed for such. There was about 8 or 10 in our company who did not sign. And didn't the tongues wag in the Soldiers Hall last night — France, Egypt, India, Italy. Dear, dear, we were going all over the world in that Hall.

Tried to get leave for Christmas at home, but was inoculated instead. Sickening sort of a job but got it over and felt a bit silly for several hours, but all right this morning except being a bit sore. Off duty today in consequence, so have a chance to print some negatives.

A good job those pictures were printed yesterday, for we have had a full parade with all possessions resulting in a change of billets. Beastly shame, knocks my pantry darkroom out of commission. We marched to the other end of town, and me and Jimmy W___ were inflicted on a couple of sister dressmakers, one of whom is a cripple. They will doubtless be very glad of our billet money, although we really have littered up their trim little parlour with our kit.

It's quite dark in the mornings now, have to fetch our days rations of meat, etc. from a back garden, wherein is the companies quarter store. Located in a greenhouse, the access thereto being via a very narrow passage and also being

Soldiers marching, followed by new recruits. 1/5th Battalion, The Gloucestershire Regiment, 1914.

dark (having to fetch rations before first parade), there are many collisions and words with other people conveying arms full of bread, meat, spuds etc.

We are now, in this new billet, only five minutes from our Soldiers Hall, but it still takes half an hour to get that wretched belt into action to go there. These sort of things will win the war but it's discipline my dear friend, discipline.

The recent inoculation put us on the French scent, which is quite strong today. The Egypt myth is quite flown now — we are but little soldiers weak.

Had mules on parade today with the transport wagons, instead of the old dobbins. Nearly took a short cut to Kingdom Come via a pair of runaway mules complete with wagon. Think our transport drivers will resign — there is a tide in the affairs of men ...

What a Christmas, the girls did very well, but I was in bed by nine o'clock on Christmas night.

The France story is going strong now, and our officer thinks it's correct, so have applied for a leave. Been reading Kipling's 'Absent-Minded Beggar'.

Splendid effort, going home for five days on Saturday — the next few parades will go well.
Am in the train, having just caught the midnight for the north. Jolly old guard, locked me in a compartment to myself saying, 'Get down and have a sleep, I'll see you change all right', decent old johnnie.

Had a good holiday, mended Em's sewing machine, patched up legs of kiddie's doll, and done umpteen jobs about the house — Tempus Fugit...

The train was on time, so easily caught the Chelmsford connection and reported at Orderly Room. All O.K.

Changed billets again today, rotten nuisance, cannot see the idea, and this is a poor place, stone floor and like a barn, but however …

Kit inspection, very thorough indeed and every button shines like a spot of gold — we really are very pretty soldiers. The reason for all this is a big parade tomorrow, and we hear that the King is coming down to see us.

Had a very heavy day. H.M. the King did arrive, we had a long march, and a longer wait; heaps of Brass Hats, piles of Staff people, scores of cars and thousands on foot like yours truly, tired of it all… Make thee mightier yet…

Got a cushy job today, moving stores to another part of the town, riding about on a four ton W.D. *[War Department]* lorry. Twelve of us to do four men's work, à la Army.

Am afraid this has been neglected, have been rather busy on guard at the high power wireless station. Oh! What did we hear, spies everywhere waiting a chance to blow it up, important people, we… They tell us this station keeps in touch with the Navy at sea, so we developed a rolling gait! Sailors don't care…

Great cheers, three bags full. Got issued with the khaki webbing equipment, and handed in the terrible leather harness. Someone is seeing sense at last, the comfort is great.

There's great excitement among the Wigs, we've been tearing about all over, and the most important event is that we have packed all our private possessions to be sent home, leaving us only the official kit and our thoughts.

29 MARCH 1915

Parade this afternoon for an unknown destination.

We are in France after all the rumours. After a very minute check of all our kit and ourselves on the station at Chelmsford, we were efficiently sandwiched into a train, and without the foggiest idea 'where to', travelling on until it got dark. We eventually stopped alongside a steamer, could just make out her lines in the darkness.

Folkestone, Dover, Plymouth, Southampton all got credited with our most respectable presence, and in half an hour we were all aboard, and under the hour we felt King Neptune wagging his trident under us. Stepping ashore at midnight, the first people to greet us was a group of Red Cross nurses, practically, very cheery and jovial, but otherwise they gave us much food for thought.

Spent the rest of the night under canvas on top of the hill at Boulogne, climbing thereto over the cobbles accompanied by a couple of small boys (at that time of night) singing snatches of Tipperary, in very broken English. Don Quixote's up to date indeed. *[A reference to* Don Quixote – Part II *by Miguel Cervantes, where, in Chapter 73, Don Quixote is accompanied to his house by two mischievous boys.]*

A memory of the 29 March 15
Crossing the Channel

A memory of the Channel crossing, with a T.B.D on either side — Folkestone to Boulogne.

30 MARCH 1915

A bit rocky this, we are on the way to somewhere in Cheval wagons, behind a kettle on wheels, after having a breakfast, obtained by operations with our bayonets on a large tin of bully, between fourteen of us.

Bundled out of the Cheval outfit last evening, had a rough bivouac, and this day have marched and marched and marched, cobbles and trees tall and thin in a never ending line, but we finally stopped at B___ *[Buckle appears to be confused here. 1/5th left Boulogne on 30 March by cattle truck for Steenvoorde].* Am about convinced that there is a bother on out here, for we have seen bunches of German soldiers going back the way we have come.

Spent the evening and night in B___ *[Steenvoorde],* inspected the few remaining shops, discovering a few pies and things (we exchanged our money on the boat). This seems like a nice town when things are normal, but now it's all littered up with soldiers and wagons and the doings of war.

31 MARCH 1915

This morning saw a convoy of wounded carried into what looked like the town hall, sort of temporary hospital. It was a sight that seems to put an outsize in full stops after 'Land of Hope and Glory'.

There was another Regiment marched through B___ *[Steenvoorde],* and amongst the rifles and cheery faces, spotted a lad from home, P. M.'s younger brother, so fell into step and gathered a lot of news during half a mile.

4 APRIL 1915

Moved on yesterday, after a parade in the morning at which we were lectured about being members of the British Army on foreign soil, sent to uphold a noble cause, etc., etc., but am afraid that 80% of us was thinking more about what there would be for dinner, which has been rather scrappy of late, but realise that it's no small job to feed 1000 men continually on the move, especially when there are others, and we are only a very minute cog in this huge machine. After the lecture we were issued with most of 100 rounds of ammunition per man. After a dry dinner we marched along the cobbles, and between the splendid trees, which are characteristic of this country. Passed and being passed by volumes of traffic, Ambulance cars, huge W.D. and other wagons, Tin lizzies, grey cars with officers etc., twos and threes of mounted troops and a smattering of civilians. Later on in the afternoon we could hear the distant rumble of big guns, and begin to think this is developing into a 'bother', that 'over in a few months' idea does not now seem so convincing.

[Meteren]
Seem to be dumped here for a day or so, seven of us at a farm, sleeping in the hayloft. The others are spread out all over the village in barns and other farms. We get into our 'bedroom' by means of a rather uncertain ladder; shall get used to the non-existence of the bottom rung but one after a bit.

We perform our ablutions in the yard to an audience of pigs and fowls, take our café au lait in mine host's kitchen, and real stuff it is to, when he makes it, and last night some of the boys were studying French with the aid of the farmer's daughter and a newspaper.

"Sisters leaving the shell shattered hunnery at Ploegsteert."

Am now in charge of a section, having been promoted to lance-corporal. Great doings at the farm, extra café all round, and a sort of impromptu concert last night, in which the star performer was the old farmer with songs of the Franco-Prussian war. He pranced around slaying imaginary enemies and ended by unearthing a bottle of vin-rouge and making all toast my chevrons with great gusto, but [I] remembered the missing rung.

Had my section outside today, and while we were halted on the roadside, a mounted officer stopped near by, one of the boys remarked how dirty and stained his tunic and breeches were. Then, as he passed close to us we suddenly realised that it was blood, there was more realisation of what is meant by war punched into our brains, than all we had read or ever been told.

Took leave of the farmer and his hayloft this morning and marched on. The guns keep getting more distinct, and we moved not in a body, but by platoons with a quarter mile or so between. Overhead are balloons and aeroplanes, the eyes of the guns which are well hidden, for we have only actually seen one battery so far. We eventually halted in this part village after being on the move all day. It's a part village for most of the cottages are a heap of stone and debris. A little way back we stopped a few minutes to help a couple of nuns, or sisters of mercy or whatever they are, to pile the remainder of their belongings on a wagon to go back the way we had just come; the poor souls were crying bitter.

7 APRIL 1915

[Bailleul, nr. Ploegsteert]
My little crowd are in a roofless, doorless, windowless cottage and the Cheval Noir estaminet opposite is down to its sign just over the doorway. We spent last evening and night in the cellar made gay with as many candles as we could purloin, ditto straw. The meals were also erratic today, for the butchers' shops are closed indefinitely, so we get bully and soup with tea-leaves, and tea with soup leaves, but we don't blame the kitchen staff. They are doing fine under new and adverse conditions.

We are not a very smart looking crowd now, our buttons are quite dull and dirty; boots have quite forgotten what Cherry Blossom stood for; we have had to remove the supporting wires from our caps, making them look like pricked balloons; the metal cap-badge is black from neglect; and all together we are very different in appearance to the glistening army that marched to church at Chelmsford on Sundays.

We have been told today that the front line trenches are about four miles away, and if we are very good we are to pay them a visit for a night and a day, just to see what things are like, but not all of us together. We go a platoon at a time and shall be distributed amongst the real soldiers. My section is the first batch to go to-night, we have to go up in the dark, or the other people may spot us, and then they MAY surrender and the bother would be over.

Transporting Beer, Belgium. April 23.15 This is how they
carry barrells from the cart to the pub. The name of the
pub is "The Black Horse". hieppe hord France.

8–10 APRIL 1915

[Ploegsteert]

Now we are in the front line, sandwiched amongst hardened regular troops, many of whom have been around here from the start. A very large wood is behind us many acres in extent, through which we came in single file, with the sharp snap of rifle fire getting more insistent as we progressed. Had a little diversion just before getting into the actual trenches, being that we had to dash across an open space of about 50 yards one at a time, and not at regular intervals, for the whole scene was lit up at erratic periods, by a sort of magnesium flare lights sent up by both sides. The first question of the two old soldiers with whom I shared a dug-out, was had I any 'fags'. The army seems to have vanished here. Half-a-dozen men carry out their job in their particular bit of trench; a couple of sentries changed every two hours; building up the trench with bags of earth, where it has been destroyed by rain or shell; digging sump holes to drain away water from the trench bottom and so lessen the mud during wet weather; fetching water for teas, struggling with a fire to boil the water, and many other jobs, but these fellows go on with the job like a bricklayer building a house, only there is no Sunday rest.

Dinner!! was not a pronounced success tonight (there are moments when one wants to be alone). Realised that the biscuits and cheese would keep until tomorrow. What a game, 8 to 10 feet below the level of the ground, cannot look out only via a piece of mirror or periscope, for the members of the Imperial Forces are only 80 yards away as the rifle spits. Have a sort of empty feeling, but not for the want of food.

No. 15 Section's Bay, in 34 Trench, at Ploegsteert Wood, Belgium. Solution in bottle for gas respiration, powder hose for dispersing gas, Sentry watching through periscope.

We are now back in our comparatively comfortable cellar, after seeing another of our platoons take our places. It was an experience yesterday, the phut of bullets, the scream of a shell, a mixed smell of damp straw, clay and boiled tea. We learnt a good deal of trench etiquette and unwritten laws, got smothered in clay and tried to understand it all.

It appears that we stay in this village of debris until all the Regiment has had 24 hours in the trench as we have. Do not see much of the other companies now, all are scattered about in cellars and other weird places. Our company seems like a little community by itself, and even then we are never all together, each platoon officer gets his orders and we carry out our own little jobs.

Have been away in the big wood the last two days relaying and repairing broken "duck boards", a sort of narrow framework like snow ladders on a roof which makes it easier to travel over the mud and soft ground, and as we have to walk on them in single file its like "ducks to the pool". The traffic on these "boards" is very heavy because all the stores and things for the trenches have to be carried over them, and without them the ground would soon be an impassable morass.

15 APRIL 1915

[Ploegsteert]
Great excitement in the company, for we, (the Regt) are going to relieve the regulars, and tonight we take complete charge of this section of the firing line. One of the platoons will stay in the wood as a supply column and bring us rations, ammunition, and other things during the 8 days we are there. We move off as soon as it gets dark.

We have now moved up into the front line, just in front of the wood edge, my little lot, 8 in all are all fixed up. 3 sentries continually ears and eyes alert over that vacant 80 yards. 3 of us share a dug-out which is about 3 feet high, 5 feet long and about 5 wide. A bag over the 'front door', which is a yard square, enables a candle to be lit inside to see to write (as now) or to get a meal. Shall have to be about all night, for have charge of this particular bit of trench. Have now made close acquaintance with the brilliant lights we have seen breaking over No-Mans Land. They are fired from a large pistol, one of which I have in my pocket now, also a supply of cartridges for same. On anything the least bit suspicious happening out in front during the hours of darkness, a shot from this pistol fired up in the air after the style of a rocket will produce a very brilliant light lasting over half a minute as it falls to the earth. It is a very useful affair, for the imagination absolutely runs riot during the darkness. The night is hardly half gone, but have used 12 or 14 cartridges already to convince the boys that there is nothing moving "out there".

There does not seem to be anyone else in the world but us eight fellows. Except an occasional messenger or an officer passing to another part of the trench, it is really amazing how quiet it all is — very queer affair, suppose the other people know we are here? Can see the sky above and the sillouetts of the sentry and that is about all. Twinkle little star, Oh I wonder...!

A member of the ration party arrived half an hour ago. He brought a lucky bag, i.e. a sandbag delivered to yours truly for my section. Contents:- a piece of raw beef, a lump of cheese, 24 'dog' biscuits [i.e. the hard biscuits issued as soldiers' rations], 2 loaves of bread, tea and sugar screwed up in a piece of newspaper, salt ditto, about 14 potatoes complete with earth, a piece of impossible bacon, a tin of Plum and Apple, and a small quantity of charcoal. This is our sustenance for the next 24 hours. Think the Savoy rather a good place to feed!

After the arrival of the rations came the order to 'stand to'. This was half an hour before daylight, and meant that every man in the trench with all his equipment, rifle and bayonet, was on parade until half an hour past daybreak. During this hour the Sergt-Major appears with a jar of rum and those that want a tot can have it. It was rather an eerie feeling, all standing together fully armed, speaking in whispers while waiting for dawn to break.

Just dished the rations out to the boys. Managed to cut up the meat (with newspaper stuck around it) into fairly equal portions with my jack knife. The cheese was easy, so was the bread, but most of the biscuits are still in the bag. Shall have to rig up some sort of cooking affair. Also water is difficult to get, have to send one of the boys a long way with an ex-rum jar. Going to curl up now for as long as possible and have a sleep ready for tonight.

"Romarin du hord, France." "French Cavalry. May 25.15."

HBB
Aug 25·15

French Cavalry.

Trust I shall have digested that bacon (plus the way we cooked it) before then — almost wish I had breakfasted on cheese and jam.

Rigged up a topping fireplace now, found some bits of iron, cut a hole in the trench side, and got a very respectable fire without smoke, for smoke attracts the people over the way and they may send over a few reminders. However, we grilled our pieces of beef, made some tea, and had a very decent meal plus clay. The Captain came along today and made some very charming remarks about our fireplace; think it must be about the best in the company by what he said.

Had an anti-gas equipment brought today, a piece of cotton wool on a tape, one for each of us to tie over the mouth, a bottle of solution to soak it in first, and a wood cigar box (at least it looks like one), filled with gunpowder with a short fuse attached. This is to be lit and thrown into the approaching gas-cloud to disperse it.

A hole cut in the clay back of the trench, and parts of a biscuit tin, made this fireplace, where six of us cooked all our meals for weeks. This Range we cut in the side of the trench (clay) the front was a biscuit tin with holes punched in, it was generally effective, but occasionally took a lot of coaxing to boil our "dixies" [i.e. kettles or pans]. This is in the trenches we were in in May & June. [The following crossed out, presumably by Buckle himself] — Dear Beck,. Note. All these water colors should be examined at least arms length away as you know. One of four.

Had a brilliant brainwave today. In last night's lucky bag discovered some flour with water and rolled into balls, boiled them well, and greatly enjoyed our cooking with the addition of some jam. After that experiment also made a pudding!! Powdered several of the "dog" biscuits, soaked them in the remains of some tea until soft, put a good dose of jam into it, stirring the whole over a fire until fairly hot — had a rare old feast. As water is scarce, utilised the dumpling water for the luxury of a shave.

It has been raining now for nearly three days, and we are getting sticky, putties and overcoat is a mass of clay-mud. We use the ground-sheets as capes. The dug-out straw is ground into the floor by crawling in and out, the wet has penetrated into everything, puddles and holes appear wherein one goes over boot-tops, but carry on as usual is the order, for boots must not be removed AT ALL while in the front line. Our water supply at the moment is quite good, for have dug a hole at the end of the traverse and it keeps full. It's a bit brown, but not bad when strained through a hanky when one can be found.

Being relieved tonight, for which many thanks. Hear we are going back about 5 miles. Suppose the folk over the way are as sticky as us. Rather jolly if we could all get out on top and shake things a bit dry, instead of creeping around down here like water rats. Am afraid none of us feel very heroic at the moment.

20 APRIL 1915

Back at a farm at R___ *[Romarin].* Had a shave this morning, taken a load from the face and the mind. This is a small farm like many others here, where a dog works a sort of treadmill to grind cattle food and the like. The whole platoon is here, and there are many exchanges of yarns and experiences in 'the doings' as the front line is called. Our officer in the house, the Sergts in the loft, and the men in the barn, everybody having a bundle of straw to make a bed (if lucky). Decent people here. Café au lait very good and cheap, and always a huge welcome in the huge parlour-cum-kitchen.

Could not sleep last night, such a peculiar smell in my corner, so being a dry night, cleared out into the orchard till morning. Borrowed a groundsheet to go with my own, and have rigged up a tent in the orchard under the trees. Have had an hour's drill, a lecture, and some clean up. Believe me, took hours to get rid of the mud and clay, and it keeps a cropping up now.

Retired into my bivouac last night and had a topping sleep. Also two officers came in the orchard with their sleeping bags, saw them settle and wished them good-night. Woke this morning with rain pouring on my tent. It was very early but the officers were gone, too wet I expect. Curled up again and was rudely wakened by two of the boys pulling the tent on top of me, so popped out and had a real wrestle with both of them. It's a great relief to have a bit of 'horse play' now and then; it counteracts the more serious matters we have in hand.

Dog wheel for Butter
aking. Belgium.

HGB Al

The Dog wheel at our Farm at Romarin. M. Jonville Page.
The dog is put in through the opening (I have shewn the
gate open). The gate is shut & the dog trots round inside the
wheel on the platform. Of course, the churn is inside the
house.

Sunday. Had an impromptu service this morning. Lt. M____ read a few verses, and we sang, 'O God Our Help', and 'Onward Christian Soldiers'. Except for the guns now and then, we seemed a long, long way from disputes. Rearrainged the bivouac this afternoon, so that one side ties up like a garden tent; spent the rest of the day (just happened to be no duty) drawing and writing.

Go back to the front line tonight. Have spent the last three days in drill, lectures, washing socks, shirts, towels and other general clean-ups. Also have got the boys to collect some dry bits of wood for our fire. If we all take a bit up with us, we should have enough to last us this time in. The wood problem to start a trench fire is very acute, for the whole place up there has been combed clear of anything that will burn, and we shall certainly want some hot tea. We parade at dusk.

We are in again, another fresh position, not quite so comfortable (save the mark) as before. Things are awfully quiet; in fact, painfully quiet in view of the fact that this is a full-blown war. Presume we are holding our own — perhaps the lull before the storm. The trench is certainly a lot drier, and if the rain keeps off we may have a pleasant time!

Have made an even better fireplace than before, a biscuit tin with holes jabbed in with a bayonet, the tin being fixed in an opening in the side of the trench. It's a fine affair. Shall be able to have some more dumplings if we can get any flour. The water is still a bother to get — have to go back to an old pump from here, and only at night, and be very careful then. Several fellows have been laid out there — they *[i.e. the Germans]* know this pump and have its range, etc.

Huge game of Chess this, we are the pawns, but no idea whose move now.

Considering there are so many of us here, we get our letters very regular. The parcels get smashed up a bit sometimes, but it's all in the game, and nobody seems to grumble such a great deal. It's wonderful how this job seems to level us all up. Several of our company who, socially are miles above lots of us, now carry a three days beard, get mucked up with clay, and wield a spade with the best. It's a bit monotonous at times, but we are never idle; there's always bits of trench to repair and strengthen.

They straffed us pretty heavy this morning, lost one of my boys, bullet clean through his head. Buried him this afternoon in the wood behind. R.I.P.

Came out last night and am now back at the farm. Found there were several other casualties. The missing boys were soon enquired for by the farm people. We have had the usual clean up, and hear that we are all going for a bath to-morrow. Ne plus ultra...

"Romarin du nord, France." "French Infantry. May 25.15."

No 7.

23 APRIL 1915

Had a georgeous day — bath, clean underclothing, tunic and all other clothes fumigated, clean everything. The whole company marched into N___ [Nieppe], to methinks, a dye works that has been now converted into a human laundry. However we all stripped to our shirts, [and] labelled our uniform with our identity disc. The uniforms, scores at a time were thrown into a sort of oven, while we went along the river bank to the wash house to four huge tubs holding seven men each. Shirts and socks were thrown into a pile, and into the tubs we scrambled like schoolboys. Grand warm water, plenty of soap. They gave us 15 minutes and then turned a cold water hose on us. Towels were ready and, when we were dry, went to a table and drew a clean shirt and socks, then back into the first building, where an R.A.M.C. [Royal Army Medical Corps] man was raking our bundles out of the oven. Yelling out the numbers, [he] hurled it at you when you answered. There were creases galore, but we were CLEAN. Had half an hour in N___ [Nieppe], then marched back. Splendid effort, good effect on body and mind.

Am orderly corporal for the remainder of this 'rest'. Up at 5am, and to reach all the platoons of the company have most of 5 miles to cover. My job is (in the mornings) to see if there is anyone reporting sick, which is the official name for all kinds of illness. A report has to be made out, and those that can, have to be at Headquarters by 8.30, and it's my job to see that they are there, to be examined by the M.O. (Medical Officer). So actually, those that are not feeling up to the mark, have to be up long before the others, and woe betide parading before the M.O. while on "rest" in an

"Mr. Mason of No. 7 Platoon."

ing apparatus in a Dye Works at N—

"The "Bath" in a Dye Works at hieppe, France. Pont de hieppe." "This is an old one (June) I have only just finished. The R.A.M.C. attendant is just flushing one lot with cold water, & the other is yelling 'Any more for any more.', a favourite cry of his to hurry us up."

unshaven state. After 'sick' parade, the Company Sergt Major gives us any orders there might be to take back to our Company Orderly Sergt. This job is a glorified messenger boy, someone to blame if anything goes wrong, and you must not answer back.

It's not a bad business being orderly after all, had a few days and rather enjoyed it. Having to be at H.Q., frequently one sees old pals of other companies. Also have a decent time to myself, but always have to be on hand, (there IS fireworks if the O. Corporal cannot be found instantly). Sort of kept on the shelf ready to be reached down and made use of.

Going back to the line to-night, but understand its farther to the left, near to M___ [Messines]. Also heard that it's not very comfortable there just at present. Going to try and find some bits of wood before we parade.

Been very busy this last few days, ditto nights more especially. We arrived here after a few encounters with shell-holes, tree-stumps, wiz-bangs, mud and bad language. Rather a poor outfit this, compared with our last time 'in'. It's like leaving a front street house for a back slum alley, for these gashes in Belgium are much lower than our friends the enemies are, and they keep spitting bits of lead at us, cannot get a bit of rest. Have to use listening posts here, 3 men out 50 yards in front of the front trench, lying in a hole reached by crawling along a shallow zig-zag cutting. A putrid sort of job, had a couple of hours at it last night; seemed like a young eternity and the rats are awfully inquisitive. Shall find grey hairs next shaving time.

An impression of the fine avenue of Bel

An attempt of an Avenue between Ploegsteert and Romarin near the French-Belgian frontier.

Dog cart for the delivery of Bread, etc. Allouagne. There [sic] dogs do a lot of hard work & *every man* has his hands in his pockets.

This is the worst trench we have struck as yet. Can now imagine what the very first troops out here had to put up with in the first trenches that were made. Can quite see that if these trenches were wider the enemy would be able to fire right into us; they nearly can as it is, they being along the hill top and we are sort of in the valley. It's extreme caution every moment we are out of the dug-out.

Relieved by the Essex Regt last night, and the poor beggars are using the old leather pouch atrocities of equipment *[i.e. the leather equipment described on pages 26 and 28]*. They are a new Regt. just come out — they have my sympathy. Had a rotten journey back, they kept biffing stuff at us. We got back before daylight however, and had a jolly good wash, the first for six days.

Planted back at the old farm, for which many thanks, for we hear there are many a great deal worse. An old melodeian arrived here today, and yours truly seems to be the only one who can knock a decent tune out of it, and I have many promises to get my rifle carried when we are out if the "band" plays. There has been nothing exciting this last 4 or 5 days, except a spy some of our fellows found all got up in khaki, only he had one shoulder number Manchester, and the other Warwicks, and no cap badge. They waltzed him off to H.Q. and have heard no more of him.

The company moved up last night into our old position, but our platoon are in what is left of a farm building in the wood, for we are the ration party this time. We start work at dusk. Today's rations were taken up by the last people. There's a nice bit of sun today, and it's very pleasant where I am now, sat on a tuft of grass with my back against the farm wall in the sunshine. Just had some tea, bread and bully plus cheese, and a slice of bread and jam, so feel personally at peace with the world.

"One of our worst "Listening Posts". We had to crawl up an old ditch, 100 yards in front of our trench. The German lines are Just below the skyline. Messines, Belgium."

"One of the French "75s" which covered us for a few weeks after relieving the French infantry." "A "75" adapted as anti-aircraft. Bayencourt, May 1915." [*The French 75mm Field Gun was probably the most effective in its class of any of the combatants during the Great War, being both rapid-firing and accurate.*]

Our "Rest" Farm at Romarin, four miles from the trenches.

One of the many Praying Shrines of France-Belgium.
Romarin. This is one of the Shrines I have told you about.
It's quite near here, the people cross themselves each time
they pass one.

Well, we have got our first ration night over. Every single item that is wanted up yonder, has to be CARRIED from the G.S. *[General Service]* wagons over two miles through this wood, right into the front line. There's food, ammunition, sandbags, timber, corrugated iron, charcoal, letters and parcels. We made 8 journeys last night, and [as] the last quarter mile is rather open, we had to rub mud on the large tins of biscuits, for they are like a mirror when a light goes up, and we have to freeze in position when it bursts until it dies down. Shall do better to-night now we know the way about. This wood and its surroundings are like a town, footways leading all over (on 'duck boards'), all complete with signposts. There's Hyde Park Corner, where the wagons come to, then Prowse Point, and Somerset House; Dead Horse Corner, not to be confused with Dead Horse Farm, and so on ad lib. When we had got all the stuff up it was getting on for daybreak, so we had to "stand to" then for most of an hour because we are also the second line of defence, or a portion of it anyway. Then [had] some bread and jam and tea. This afternoon we are busy making stretchers and carriers, and we hope that with these, two men will carry as much as three or more did last night.

Had a glorious meal today, got a Maconachie ration from some engineers in the wood, a round tin containing meat, spuds, carrots, beans and gravy, enough for two in a tin. This is the first time we (the poor infantry) have seen one, had a real blow out, must try and get another. They are the goods, believe me!

Got back to the farm again, been awfully busy this last few days. Our Brass Hats would decide on fresh trench additions, renovations etc., when WE are on the ration party. Should think we have slugged tons of timber and iron sheets up to the front for the aforesaid renovations. It turned out to be a real hefty job; all my boys say they would rather be in the front.

Had a fairly easy day today, nothing much but personal cleanliness. A bevy of Brass Hats descended on us this afternoon, and ticked some of us off because the salute was not smart, and because some mud was shewing here and there, but they did not know that many putties were slipped off and put back inside out. Mud out of sight is out of mind. Have heard a lot recently about London buses conveying troops about, but all our movements since the train has been in the same pair of boots.

The laundry people have not called yet, must ring them up(!) for this is the same shirt obtained from the great bath at N____ [Nieppe].

Had a bit more drill today. Must not forget how to form fours, very necessary in a trench 3 feet wide... [i.e. a column of fours, a formation used when a unit marched four men abreast, primarily for road marching. Henry is being sarcastic.] Wonder if the other people are doing the same things. It's getting a sort of settled affair now; in the "doings" for 5 or 6 days, then back here for a few days to scrape the mud off. It may be for years and it may be forever!

Half a dozen N.C.O.s from our company, including myself, are to go back about six miles tomorrow, to talk to a fresh Regt just arrived. Have to tell them what the front line is like, what we do and how to do it, and goodness knows what else. We six have had a lecture ourselves about it — what we have to say in general, morale, esprit de corps and all the rest of it.

Am now about ten miles from the front, with one of the fresh Regts from England. There has been constructed here about 200 yards of trench in facsimile of the firing line, complete with barbed wire, dug-outs, traverses and all the other impedimenta except the sticky mud. It's a nice, clean

Rations
Ploegsteert Wo...

"Every single thing for the trenches had to be _carried_ from the A.S.C. [Army Service Corps] wagons, through the wood, nearly two miles. Ploegsteert."

a row of rough Dugouts at "Prowse Point". Ploegsteert Wood. These dugouts are just behind the firing line, and are made of bags of earth, trees, biscuit tins, and are bullet and shrapnell proof, limbs of trees on top, to prevent them being seen by enemy aircraft. Prowse Point, Ploegsteert.

Belgian Refugee
77.

A poor old
chap from
Arminteers,
[Armentières]
whose remains
of furniture
we helped to
move. Drawn
from life in
a farmhouse
at Romarin,
Dep. Du
Nord, France.

Sunday trench all dressed up and nowhere to go, but, however, we 6 N.C.O.s get a crowd of these good fellows who have come out here to help, and we impart to them what we have seen and know, explaining trench etiquette with practical illustrations. It's a great game, and a jolly good rest for us fortunate six.

We were hiked back this afternoon just in time to catch up with our own crowds at Hyde Park Corner, and get back in the front again, in our old place where we were first of all. There has been many improvements made since we were here last. Prowse Point is quite nice and clean and passable, new "duck boards" all over the place, extra signs and direction boards up so that one cannot get lost. Somebody HAS been busy... Oh, it's a pretty war!

Just below us, in the next section, the people across the way have an erection, which we call the 'birdcage', a sort of squat fort built with sandbags, wherein are a few machine guns, which annoy us very much indeed. Our Engineer people are going to remove this tomorrow, (Sunday) for understand they (the Engineers) have tunnelled across to it and placed a few bags of explosive right underneath. ... All day today the gentlemen of a mountain, or mortar battery, have been yanking their infernal machines along our trench to a position opposite the 'birdcage', and a Machine Gun Section are with us here and, if you please, are going to plant their apparatus alongside our dugout, so that they can add to the din when the balloon , i.e. 'birdcage', goes up. It's all very well that, but the other folk will locate this Machine Gun, and will be putting some stuff across here, and WE are here for a day or so yet — the good Gunners will be gone when their job is done.

Ploegsteert Wood. A faint impression of the bursting of a Shrapnell Shell. May 31.15

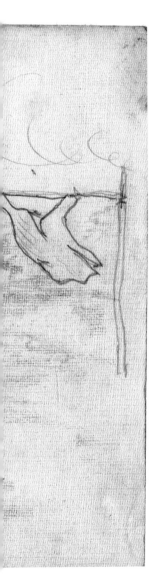

"Explains itself." "Washing Day.
Whit Sunday 1915."

On the way from 'Hyde Park Corner' to the front line trench. Ploegsteert, Belgium. I have had to cut this down a bit. The lines tied to the sign post are field telegraph wires. Names on signpost are given to different routes on all the tracks. I have been by this corner scores of times.

6 JUNE 1915

Had a very noisy and strenuous day. The 'birdcage' went up as per schedule, and is now scattered over the surrounding country. The noise was terrific, and they spat at us all along the line, all sorts of stuff: rifle grenades, wizzbangs and Dickens knows what else. In fact they are on yet, and it's past midnight but, of course, if you do tickle anyone, they do not usually sit quite still. There are no casualties in my little lot so far, although we were all 'standing to' while the fireworks were going. This sort of affair means scrapp meals; job to boil water for tea and all that sort of thing. Not good for us, you know.

The Regt (or whatever they call themselves) opposite to us are very keen. An instance, we have in the front parapet oblong holes about the size of a brick, through which we look and fire when necessary, although it's usual to look over the top by the aid of a periscope, it's safer. One of these holes is half-way down a cul-de-sac where a sentry is posted. All sentries are visited about every quarter hour. I had just been to this one and, coming back, at the hole a bullet took several hairs from the back of my head between cap and collar. Reckon the johnny opposite saw me pass down, and waited for the return, but he was a fraction of a second too late. A miss is as good as a few meals, and it's all in the day's stickiness.

Back at the jolly old farm again. M'sieur Y___ P___ is still tending his cattle and chickens, and I am still lodging in the orchard. We are like bagatelle balls, on the table for a bit, then into the pocket for a rest.

"A German Sandbag Fort called "The Birdcage", opposite
"Plugstreet" wood. We blew this up with a mine on Sunday
June 6.15"

Had a very nice 'rest', and going up tonight into the reserve line in St I___ [*Yves*] village, or what's left of it. Have collected the usual bits of dry twigs for a fire, and packed all our possessions, as we always do, for we never know where we shall come back to. All movements are uncertain, and what one does not carry with us, we do not have.

Am now in the village of St I___ [*Yves*], dividing my time between 'Warwick Castle' and the Post Office, or what is left of these two once auspicious buildings. Cannot stroll up the street; have to jump into a 6 foot trench to fetch the morning milk (great joke). What used to be the doorway of the Post Office is all smashed up with Machine Gun bullets, and the Office proper is minus its front walls. They are built upon a bit with sandbags, and there is a sentry keeping watch by the aid of a periscope. Warwick Castle, where the other half of the platoon are now residing, is even worse; there are only a few bricks remaining and the cellar is the bed-cum-dining room.

We are employed during spare time in rebuilding and strengthening the village trenches, keeping the way clear to the front line. There's always chunks of wall falling down to be cleared away, and each Battalion C.O. has his pet idea as to how a trench should be. Hence we are constantly removing Belgium from here to there, and there to somewhere else.

There is no official business done at the Post Office now; the only stamps are made with our feet. Orders are obtained from the C.O. There is telegraphic communication certainly, but it is a private wire to the Field Battery in our rear.

"Warwick Castle", St Yves village, Ploegsteert. We occupied
the cellar of this "castle".

View from the Post Office.
'May 30 - 15   FLB

The Post Office at "St Ives". The enemy held the village on the skyline. Tobacco leaves hanging from the beam on the right. The German trenches are directly in front. A sentry is looking over the sandbags with a periscope. The brown stuff hanging from the beam on the right is tobacco leaves, drying. Church & town in distance. The top of this building is completely smashed in by shell fire.

Have presumably left our dear old farm at last, for we are now come out of 'reserve' and are back in a very large farm, big enough to hold the whole company, right back among the Brass Hats. My little lot are in a corner of a sort of grannery, and just outside is a large pond, chocked with weeds and rubbish and, what is far worse, swarmed with rats. Last night we had to roll ourselves right up in the blanket, head and all, (we had a blanket issued each on arrival), for dozens of these rodents, during most of the night, played tig, ring o' roses, and ran obstacle races over us.

Have seen no civillians here so far, suppose we are still too near the business end of war, although it seems far enough a way to us. Had to take my boys to clean up a chateau today; orders were that a staff officer would come here and take us to it. Paraded at the appointed time and waited, continually coming to the salute for passing officers, and it was nearly two hours before our man turns up, and on a horse at that. 9 fellows waiting 2 hours for one man. Had *we* been two minutes late, eh? Fireworks! He leads us off still on his horse, about a couple of miles to the chateau. Quite a nice place, lots of furniture still left in, looked as if the owners had made a very hurried departure. It is evidently going to be a Staff Office of some sort.

Ploegsteert Wood. The enemy, and our trenches can be seen on the left of the wood. The German Trenches are the white line of sandbags on the left of the wood. Guns are the dark line lower down. The communication trench to the Post Office is just in the foreground.

We gave the place a good tidy up, to the satisfaction of 'his nibs', and he sent us back to the rats.

Moving tomorrow, shall have to be up early. Also, shall not have my rifle carried, as in the past, for someone has trod on the band and bust its bellows, so shall have to regretfully leave it to the rats; but all the same think the boys are getting a bit tired of 'Land of Hope and Glory', and 'Little Grey Home in the West'. There are great doings in 'the office' tonight; think it's a big move.

Have marched umpteen kilos today, and am now parked up in an open field, and it's raining hard. Just rigged up a bit of shelter with ground sheets. In for a bad night, can't write any more.

Have heard we are in for a long march. Have had a dry up in the sun, which broke out this morning; going to get a sleep this afternoon. We move off at dusk.

"A Bivouac of myself and a pal, on our Journey down the line. Chocques, near Bethune." "Our bivouac on the 26-27 June 15 under a partly fallen tree at C___. June 27.15."

16/17 JULY 1915

Very long march last night, kept on till nearly daylight. We are all together now, that is, the whole Battalion. Heaps of troops about. Met several Battalions during the night, some of them were Canadians, quite a lot of back-chat as we passed one another. Seems to be our move now in this great game. Had a good sleep this morning and am ready for tonight. Don't know where we are, but it seems a nice town, quite a number of people about, although the manhood between 17 and 50 is conspicuous by its absence. My little lot slept in an outhouse of a large mansion, which has some lovely gardens.

Have not bothered to write or draw this last few days, too tired marching all night, then sleep, orderly and Regimental routine fills up the day very completely.

Wish we were marching in daylight. This seems very nice country, with its grand trees, canals and quaint bridges over them, but cannot see much, its just crunch, crunch and keep in step, with your eyes on the fellows pack in front. We have a bit of a song now and then, but not allowed to make too much noise.

Halted right in the country this morning, me and a pal rigged up a nice bivvy under a tree. Had a real swagger wash in a stream just by, then a good sound sleep and feel quite bucked again.

"An item in our long "trek" from the Ypres district to the Somme district, marching each night. The above is when nearing our billet village (after a very wet night) at 3am in the morning. Ames, France." "On this occasion we were marching from 9 at night until 4 in the morning, I never appreciated STRAW so much in my life."

Had a surprise last night, did not go very far, but spent the rest of the night in a sort of huge shed which seems to be used for the drying of hops or something like that. There are scores of long poles over our heads on racks, and the sides of the shed are latticed. It's a concrete floor, and it struck very cold last night, so have tied a dozen poles together on their rack to sleep on. It will be all right if they don't roll, [as] they are 10 feet from the concrete floor!

Stayed here last night, expect they don't want to knock us all up, for several are with the R.A.M.C. mostly groggy about the feet.

Moved on again, in daylight this time, and not so far before platoons broke off different ways to various farms. Whenever our platoon gets by itself it seems yours truly has to be the interpreter, go into the farm first, and find out where we are to sleep, where the officers are to go, borrow spades, and so on; and when we strike a village there's shopping for the boys, buying apples, cherries, etc. whenever we have the opportunity.

A German Shell (H.E.) bursting against the Engine House of a Colliery at L—.
July 16.15.

'We were uncomfortably close while this colliery was being "straffed". They attended to us after, but we luckily had only one casualty in our Platoon. Loos, France." "We watched this mine being shelled with high explosive shells & Just after were shelled ourselves with shrapnel. July 16.15."

17 JULY 1915

Again we have moved, and this is the village of A___ [Ames]. Not a very good sleeping berth for my lot; it's a concrete floor again, but we are together, the 8 of us. The tenant is very good, found us some straw and bags, so have made things fairly decent.

Think we must be lost or forgotten, been here four days now, doing a bit of drill, scouting lectures, and seem to be just filling up time. Madame here is very good to us, her husband is at the front, and she is running the little farm. Her brother comes to help now and then, he is a miner and had a long talk with him last night. Shewed my sketches and had an interesting time together.

Had a 10 mile march today, lined the road near L___ [Loos] for the Prince of Wales and Lord Kitchener to pass. They did not stop to speak, just nodded as they passed, but very pleased to see them out here. We went back in the afternoon to our concrete floor, and had a go at slinging up a hammock with a ground sheet, it will not be so hard as the concrete, providing that the strings hold good.

18 JULY 1915

Sure we are forgotten, been here now 7 days, still drilling about and spend the evenings in Madame's kitchen sipping her adorable café au lait, and holding impromptu concerts to which she and her two kiddies listen with great glee and laughter. She listens to our conversation for the word "nose" and thinks it's an awfully funny word. Have just heard that we are to parade early, possibly for a move. Am just going to Company H.Q. to find what orders for the morning, leaving the boys in the kitchen singing and generally making themselves happy.

Was up early today. Marched to a railway siding, climbed into Cheval wagons, was bumped and shunted about for an hour or so. Disgorged ourselves outside a good-sized town, took to the road again alongside a river until our Company halted in the village of S____ [Sarton]. My word, what a to-do! Found that these people had not had British troops in the place before, think they were disappointed we were not kilties [i.e. Scottish Highlanders]. Wanted to examine rifles, shoulder straps, cap badges, and were generally interested. I spent a free hour sketching the quaint church, and before I had finished think most of the village had gathered round. Our night quarters is a hay loft, but nowhere and nothing decent to wash in, so scouted off up a side lane in search of same. Found the local vetinery surgeon's place and asked his good lady if we may wash at her pump. Presto! Bowl, warm water, soap, towel all appeared like in the Arabian Nights. After a good clean up had to go inside. The V.S. himself had turned up; he got out a map:. Where was the Regt from? Where was my home? Had I ever been in the great city of Londres [London], and questions galore, finishing up with inviting me to join them at their evening meal at 8 o'clock. Thumbs up, visions of pudding, pastries and perhaps vegetables.

Had an awful shock last night; had orders to take my section on a detour of a few miles to a large house to be used as Divisional H.Q. there to clean out a few rooms for our Brigade people. This meant goodbye to my evening meal. Managed to dash up to tell them, they were even more disappointed than I was. Gathered it was to have been as "posh do", but got some apples and goodies. Paraded at 8pm and got away; found the house and have made ourselves comfortable till morning, when we do our job, after which, go on again and catch the Company at S___ [Sarton] if we don't get lost. We could just as easily have come here in the morning as tonight. 'The best laid schemes of mice and men gang aft agley'.

Have had a few rather hectic days, shall have to go back a bit. We did our cleaning job at Div. H.Q. and had a splendid tramp to S____ [Sarton], and found that the company had been there for some time. They had saved a meal for us, which we promptly removed and I settled down to sleep in someone's outhouse, when the orderly Sergt comes in to warn me to parade at 5 in the morning for special duty. Seem to be catching it just lately but, however, had a good sleep and was out in the morning. It was a wee parade; myself, another corporal, two Sergts, and Lieuts, all from other companies. We were told we had been selected for our knowledge of the language (sorry for mine) and that we are now going up into the front line at present occupied by a French Regt who are being relieved by ours tonight. Our job is to spend the day with them, learn the geography of the particular section which our Companies will take over, and gain any useful information. Climbing into a G.S. wagon we were driven off. A beautiful morning — sun shining, birds singing and really delightful. Most of three miles brought us into the village of H____ [Hébuterne], another partly smashed up hamlet. We had a terrific reception, many of the French rank and file had not seen a 'Tommy' before. They swarmed all over us; 'the

"Drawn during a short rest at Allouange, France." "Note.
This was *not* drawn from life. July 15."

"I drew the above, from the steps of the Village Pub opposite, having an audience of French soldiers, we were the first British troops they had seen. Sarton, France." "I had a good look round this church, very nice to the eye, decorations are most elaborate, paint & plaster galore, altho in the chancel were 3 rather nice frescos."

war was over', 'they were going home'. The excitement was very great. We could not do or find out anything for a couple of hours.

After the preliminaries were over and the excitement somewhat abated, and they were used to the look of us, we were escorted into the front line trench. It was rather amazing to find at the end of the village street, immediately before we turned into the trench proper, a shop in which were many articles for sale, including cage birds, and almost next door a cook shop, of sorts admitted, but there it was. Except for the uniforms and the litter of warfare, we may have been tourists. However, the trench began in an orchard, where they had hoped to get some apples when ripe, via bursting shrapnel. Here we broke up into parties and Sergt R____ of the ____ Rgt led yours truly into the stretch which was detailed to be occupied by my Company at dusk. Had we left the war behind? Not a sound except the birds, and the hum of insects in the sunshine; a sentry here and there but most of the 'soldats' were busy making aluminium rings from shell parts. There were many tiny 'benches' and improvised vice to hold the ring while polishing or shaping. Many were really excellent work both in design and quality. The Sergt explained the various positions, range (150 yards to the opposite wood where our 'friends were'), the dugouts, exposed points, one especially to cross the main road. We spent a long time at this with frequent interruptions, the chief one being, 'when will the war be over?' On the way back to the Sergts' mess we passed a row of huge barrels complete with taps. Found they were Vin Rouge, which is served out liberally to the French troops. At the mess (in a part cottage) the others of our party were waiting for us, and we all sat down to a real table and also what proved to be the finest meal I had in the Army. We could not have been more than 1,000 yards from the enemy. There would be 12 of us at the table, with two waiters (Sergts' batmen) in attendance,

French Machine Gun firing on a Taube.

"The necessary tilt is obtained by fixing the gun in a special stool. Allouange." "French Machine gun firing on a Taube – July 26 1915." "Dear Beck, this gun which we saw was an ordinary Field Machine gun, mounted on a wood stand in order to get a more upright position. This is the Field Service Dress of the French Infantry, a kind of Sky Blue. Examine this at arm's length away." *[The Taube was a German monoplane, its shape well illustrated by Henry as a tiny silhouette in the top right-hand corner.]*

soup, fish, a roast, real vegetables, tinned fruit with custard, cheese, and coffee as only the French can make it, and to crown all was produced an unopened bottle of Black and White, where on earth from puzzles me to discover. We had a real royal time with no interference and no-one to say nay, the whole being beautifully cooked and plenty of it.

At dusk we moved to the end of the village to await the Battalion, which duly arrived to time. The Companies broke up and were led by us to their various trenches, of which we fore-runners had assimilated the geography thereof. There was another great 'to-do' when our fellows got amongst the Frenchmen. Altho it was dark, there were gifts of rings and souvenirs, and after many hand-shakes they left us.

My little section occupy the orchard trench, and these people certainly knew of the change in events (that is the people over the way) for we had not been in 24 hours before they strewed shrapnel all over the place. ... The occupants on this side must have thought it was a permanent war, for this trench is real "posh", floored with bricks in many places, neat little dug-outs lined with straw, and nearly all fitted with doors.

"Another part of the trenches we took over from the 93rd Regt. of French Infantry." "An idea of part of the Trench taken over from the French on 20 July 1915." "This part exactly faces the famous Gommercourt [Gommecourt] Wood".

An Idea of part of the French taken over from the French on 20 July 1915.

HGB
July 22 .15

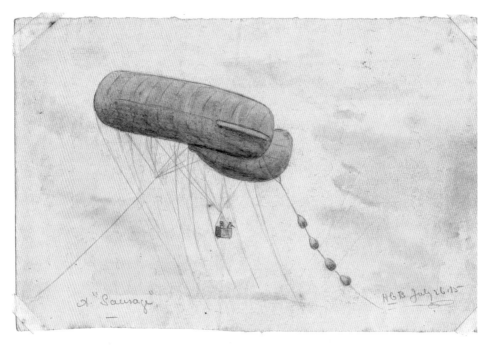

A "Sausage".

HGB July 26 15

"An Artillery Observation Ballooon, drawn with the aid of field glasses at Bayencourt." "This is the type of observation Balloon in use by the Germans, this particular one is quite near us and is now used by the French, if there was a captured one from the Germans, I do not know! — Hold it at arm's length! — We call them "Sausages".

This morning while on duty in the orchard, our Brigadier appears. He is a jolly little round chap, almost as tall lying down as standing. After plying me with questions about our new trenches etc., he asks for the Co. *[Commanding]* Officer's dug-out. As this was some distance along, I offered to escort him to it, but "No, certainly not, corporal. You must stay and carry out your duties. I'll find it alright", says he. But he had not gone 30 yards when they put over a couple of wizz-bangs. Your humble was flattened out at the first whine as per habit [and], after the bits had ceased falling, looks round for the Brigadier. He was groveling in the only sticky bit of trench around here, [so] ran and helped him up. " I think, Corporal", says he, "you had better show me your C.O.'s dug-out after all, and as quick as possible", which order was duly carried out.

Have now moved back into H_____ *[Hébuterne],* and am quartered in what was the village pub, my little lot being in occupation of the bar parlour. Quite a comfy spot as things go here. Had time for a look around this afternoon. They have certainly levelled it a bit; the Church is gone except one arch which looks ready to fall. In fact there are many 'Prenez Guarde' *[Prenez Garde – 'Take care']* notices about, also saw the A.S.C. people are very busy filling a large barn with tins of bully and biscuits, loads of it. Not a healthy sign, methinks.

Another thing our people are doing, the 'bird' shop is gone, also the shop next door to it. In fact all civillians are cleared out, and there were quite a few. One dear old lady had to be positively carried from her cottage. She was not ill, just did not want to leave. Think our folk mean to stir up the peaceful aspect of this village and its surroundings.

Our home for 8 days, 1500 yards from the Germans.

"The most homely billet we ever had, altho we were "straffed" daily. Hebuterne." "Our home for 8 days, 1500 yards from the Germans. Aug. 8.15." "You will see the "Rowntrees" box on the cupboard, in the right bottom corner you will see our beds, straw, divided by boards, the table under the window is one I rigged up with a door, also note the dog, a nice little thing which was here when we came, we washed him yesterday & gave him a dose of "Keatings" & he's quite smart, we call him "Rations". — Opposite Gomercourt [Gommecourt] Wood." [N.B. Keating's Flea Powder]

Was out with a wiring party last night in a rather exposed position, could not risk hammering the stakes in to carry the vine, just had to push them by main force, and all the time the frequent 'pings' over our heads told us that the others had an idea someone was about. Had a sleep this morning and have been digging a communication trench this afternoon.

What a silly 'do' last night! Our platoon had orders to parade at the village pond at 11pm, when someone from H.Q. would come along and give us instructions as to what we were to do. At about 11.30 it rained, and rained, and poured, thunder, lightning and all the rest. We were soon soaked through, and it still rained and we still waited until 2 am, when our officer managed to get in touch by telephone with H.Q., who said they thought it was too damp for the job. It was, and it had taken them 3 hours to find it out. We had a Dickens of a job to 'dry up'; some of my gear is not dry now.

We are now moved on to the second line of defence, that is, as far as our platoon is concerned, in the occupation of a farm about half a mile in rear of the front line. It's QUITE a nice farm, as war farms go. My section occupies the huge kitchen. The roof of the building is a mass of debris filling up the rooms over us, so we are only using the ground floor. It is not healthy to get any higher. The kitchen is very nice — a grandfather clock, a large dresser, a table, and a dog, a nice little chap who is friends with everybody. He won't leave the place so gets fed and looked after by the various platoons in occupation. I hope the little fellow will be all right somewhere if a real row starts around here. One excellent thing is a pump in the yard which is still in commission, so for the time being we can perform our ablutions in frequency and comfort, with an occasional scramble when someone wants the only pail to wash shirt and socks, etc.

Our bit of trench exactly facing Gomercourt [Gommecourt] Wood, the sentry on left is firing into the wood, near him is the Rocket Apparatus used by the French. Hebuterne.

BOYAU DES ARTILLERS

Our portion of trench on
30 July 1st Aug. 15
1st 6 B.

Women working in the fields between Bus-les-Artois and Sailley-au-Bois. The barbed wire is on our second line of defence. The women were working Just in front of us, when we were fixing the barbed wire entanglements on the reserve lines. A Shell is bursting over the trees in the village of H____ [Hébuterne] and an Ambulance is on the road to S____ [Sailly-au-Bois]. The defence behind Hebuterne.

Our 'friends' have certainly woke up since we have been here, for the shelling here and to our rear is increasing daily. The main road we traversed in a G.S. wagon when we first came up is now unsafe, and all spare troops are busy digging a communication trench right away back to S____ *[Sarton]*. We have had several turns at it.

The pen is mightier than the sword, but at present the spade is a better implement than the rifle, altho the rifle is a constant companion, sleeping and waking. Don't think we shall be without one, forever and ever? It accompanies us when resting, digging, eating, on a message, or a chat with friends; its formation and shape will be engraved on our minds to the end of time.

We are now moved into the worst front line trench we have had so far, very shallow, no dug-outs. When our time for rest arrives we tuck ourselves on a sort of shelf cut in the trench side. Sometimes you 'stay put', sometimes you don't. We are at the far end of the village beyond the cemetery. The meals are much better now, for there are cooker wagons attached to each Company. Of course, they are way back in the village, nearly 2 miles away, and a ration party brings up huge 'dixies' of hot soup, tea etc., for which we are grateful beyond any expression of mine. After 'grilling' raw meat over charcoal, and boiling any old water over sticks for tea, it is indeed very comforting.

This is a rather troublesome trench. We get a lot of bother from hand grenades. Lost several fellows that way, but most of them will be replaced soon, for we hear a draft is waiting to join us when we go back a bit, which I hope will be soon, for I and all of us are very tired. There is nowhere here to rest for an hour; it's just night and day and Sunday straight on, on your feet practically the whole time.

Have been relieved now and am back right to S___ B___ [Sailly-au-Bois] where we found our draft of new men waiting for us, so have filled up the gaps left by casualties. This is not a bad village, far enough back for shops to carry on, estaminets open and, with restrictions, it's 'business as usual'. But the best thing is that we have the prospect of a BATH, for there are some long tin baths in the schoolhouse and our R.A.M.C. people are busy fixing up a boiler affair to heat the water. Very splendid! We are in a barn affair, not too bad, seems like cattle byres, but nearby is an orchard, and it's forbidden fruit, but there are a few choice pears in MY haversack. Darkness covers a lot of sin.

We are doing the usual digging and reserve defence work while back here, and today when about 3 miles out my foot went groggy, so was left to get back quietly. I was sat on the roadside answering sympathetic questions from passing villagers, when our transport people came along. They gave me leg up on a horse. Ye gods, what a journey! There was a leg at every corner but I wanted several more, what with being bareback, [carrying] a rifle, and not having ridden for many years. Had a job to stay on, but did so and rode right up to the farm in triumph amid the cheers of the assembled troops, and assured them from my seat that I had not been promoted G.O.C. [General Officer Commanding]

Got put on a day's rest yesterday, so was fit to go up again last night. Am detailed this time with my little crowd for ration duty. We occupy a large dug-out half way between the front line and our cookers in the village of H____ [Hébuterne]. Our day today has been to be at the cookers early enough to get coffee to the Company at daybreak, then back for the breakfast of tea and bacon. As this is of course in bulk and in covered tins and dixies, it keeps respectably hot during our two miles through the communications trenches.

"The East End of the Church at Hebuterne, as I last saw it, since then it has been almost levelled." "This Church is in an awfull ruin, almost beyond imagination. The pulpit is still there, not so bad, I have shewn a portion of it through the centre window, the inside of the Church was painted & might have been rather pretty, Columns & Capitols of plaster, painted. Hebuterne Church."

"The finish of our Journey south. Hebuterne, opposite Gomercourt [Gommecourt] Wood." "Part of the Village of H___ [Hébuterne]. July 29.15" "This is not a very good one."

Ruined Shrine
at H.
Aug 21.15
HGB

"A ruined shrine near our trenches. Hebuterne." "Note the bullet marks in the stone. In the foreground is a trench to the firing line. Tree limb broken off with shell. Barbed wire across the road, behind the "Tommy". Hebuterne."

When we have been down again for letters, and parcels, stores etc., then a journey with ammunition, it's time to get the dinner up. So it goes on. Time for sleep comes between tea and midnight. It's an awful soggy job at present. In fact, my chaps discard putties and socks, rolling up their trousers above the knee, wearing boots alone.

During a spare half hour today we have explored some old German dug-outs. What 'posh' affairs, rather deep down with corridors, and bunks built up with wood and canvas; real good spots, but no use to us, being a good way from our lines. Coming back cannoned into a General and his A.D.C. [Aide-de-Camp] Don't often see these chaps. He was quite chatty, asking a number of questions; in fact so pally thought he may ask me to dinner, but nothing doing...

One of our Sergts came back from a week's leave in England today, says he had actually had a ride to the rail-head in a motor-bus. Also farther back are Y.M.C.A. huts with coffee and biscuits, concert parties, and all the amenities of civilised soldiering. We have seen none of these, and he also tells us there's a rumour of a sort of steel cap or helmet, to minimise the risk of bullet or shrapnel singeing our hair.

27 SEPTEMBER 1915

Have just done another five days in the front, during which lost a great friend and pal, Lieut. M___ [Moore], and several others as well. Had a raid, sort of preliminary to a big affair that is soon coming off. There were heaps of fireworks. Got our Sergt in from amongst it, and he was properly beat, shook him right up. Had to make his report out for him, piecing it together from his spasmodic remarks. Land of Hope and Glory.

"One of the many road Barricades constructed by the French
Troops. Hebuterne." "A Hebuterne Barricade. — Aug. 1915."
"Dear Beck, One of many barricades in H____ [Hébuterne]."

...of a Farm
Aug. 28.15
HGB

"This was drawn, during intervalls with the Ration Party, our Cooks were billeted here while we were in the front line. The washing basin is a Jardineer. Hebuterne." "Remains of a farm at H___ [Hébuterne]. Aug. 28.15" "On the Right, the Cellar Entrance still stands, being built of brick & cement. The Jardineer, which the "Tommy" is washing in, is a very nice one, & quite sound. — Hebuterne. — This paper is excellent."

"The Village Crucifix on the cross roads, the figure is life size. Bayencourt." "There are a great many of these crosses to be seen over here, various forms & patterns, some constructed in iron, but mostly a wood cross & a wood or plaster figure, the whole being very gaudily painted, & surrounded by trees or bushes, which are kept trimmed (or were) & carefully attended to. — Hold at arm's length."

At present we are back in another village, B_____ [Bus], and our platoon is quartered with the Company cooker so our meals are right on the spot. Just outside is the village well; the local people have taken away the large bucket affair from the chain that winds the water to the surface, so we have to get it up as best we can. The usual method is to hook an empty biscuit tin on, this comes back sometimes, but am sure that well is half full of tins by now. Have had very heavy work this "rest" building very strong defence lines. In some places using small trees whole, barbed wire, huge posts and the inevitable spade. Our people don't mean to leave here in a hurry. The whole place is now gouged up with trenches of second and third defence lines.

Went up to S___ [Sailly?] for the long-wanted bath, rather good, piles of soap, the R.A.M.C. have certainly made a good job of it. 8 tin baths in a row, hot water from a boiler outside passed in pails through a window, ditto the cold. Wood troughs on the floor and running outside saves time in emptying the bath, and over all is the delightful aroma of steam and soap, which can be only really appreciated when one has been separated from clothing only once in a month or so.

"The East End of Hebuterne near the Cemetary." "Hebuterne.
This End of the Village is an awful mess. The sign on
the right (Merci) means "Thank you", it's an advert for
somebody's motor tyres. Not much to be thankful for now,
is it."

Civilian Dugouts
at S^t. au B.
Aug 25-15   4618

"Dugouts cut by the inhabitants for their own safety, when
the shelling became "too thick". Sailly-au-Bois." "These
Dugouts are constructed by Civilians themselves as a place
to fly when the village is bombarded. How would *you* like
to have places like ths to *exist* in. This is quite true, the
pram I saw there, also the kiddies. Sailly-au-Bois."

Breakfast for the Firing Line, 2 miles away.

"This is the entrance to the long communicator, to our trenches, near the Cemetary Gates. Socks and Putties were discarded in wet weather for this Journey by the Ration Parties. Hebuterne." "Breakfast for the firing line, 2 miles away. Aug. 30." "This is as big a Job as No. 8 has had for some time. All rations cooked in the village & *carried* 2 miles to the company in the fire trenches. When wet the chaps discarded socks & putties, water & mud galore. This particular spot is the entrance to the communication trench, against the Cemetery Gates. — Hebuterne. — Road to trench facing Gomercourt [Gommecourt] Wood."

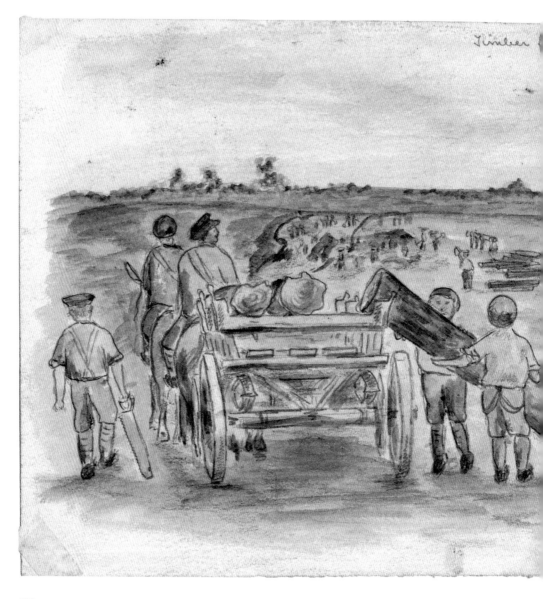

'When out of the trenches, this is how we were employed, on reserve trenches and dugouts, often work of a heavy nature. Bus-les-Artois." "Timber for Dugouts on Reserve Lines Sep. 8.15." "This Job is not all drill & trench duty. This is a Job we very often get, to assist the Engineers in reserve line works, & their necessary dugouts & communication trenches."

"Interior of a French Dugout occupied by eight of us. We built the stove (on the right) with tins etc, but was not quite successful, having to get outside while it burned up. Hebuterne." "Interior of French Dugout Aug. 29.15." "Dear Beck, This is a much better dugout than is generally the case, we have to get into most of them on our knees, I can stand nearly upright in this one. The black affair on the right is a stove? & mixed arrangement of biscuit, Jam & other tins. I may mention the chimney was *not* a success. Hal."

Interior of French Dugout, Aug 29, 15: H63

Our Billet on Sept 18. '15 HLB

"One of our Billets, my spot was where the window is marked X. hote the washing. Hebuterne." "I was sleeping in the house on the right where the window is partly filled with loose bricks, to keep the bits of shrapnell from flying in. — Hebuterne Village."

We hear there are a number of Batteries of Artillery moved up in our vicinity, but we don't bother very much, our time is fully occupied with our own job. Most of the time there to spare is spent in sleep whenever possible. Eat, sleep and be merry, for tomorrow we go back to the front line.

Have had rather an hectic time this last 6 days, and a pretty rotten time for the other people into the bargain as well, for our Artillery have been shelling their line for 4 of the 6 days. A nearly continuous scream of shell over our heads, dense masses of yellow smoke, following the repeated explosions. There were clouds of earth, heaps of timber and earth going skywards, but as soon as a lull came they would give us bursts of machine gun fire, then our guns would open again and the sky be blotted out with yellow and black smoke and dirt. One really felt sorry for the fellows there who had to stick it out and it made me wonder if after all there was not some other way to settle these disputes between nations. We had all our sentries and posts doubled with reserve Companies close at hand. They pitched a few shells into us, but the majority went behind, evidently trying to silence our Batteries. A shell burst on our dug-out, but we were all out so no human damage was done. They rousted us pretty soundly. When we were relieved and were getting away from it, there were many dives for shelter to escape flying shrapnel, and it took us a long time to get away, but eventually nearly all arrived at B____ *[Bus]* again.

We are now busy constructing more defences, working late, and a bit of straw on the barn floor is absolutely the sweetest thing on earth, when one can lie down, relax and sleep.

Our little lot have done a lot of work these last few days, and are for the "doings" again tonight for 4 days. Going up later than usual to avoid any repetition of times of relief for they do get to know these things somehow. It's rather wonderful to me. We have generally relieved about dusk, but it will be midnight this time as things are at present. By the sound of it there is still a lot of stuff flying about up yonder, but nothing like the inferno of several days ago.

OCTOBER 1915

Henry Buckle was injured on 10 or 16 October

Shall have to go back for a few days, for I am now lying in the barn with a damaged leg, the result of being too near a bursting shell. No flesh wound, but got sort of buried in the trench and twisted up. This happened two days ago, and as our stretcher people were busy told them we could manage, for I had in company Sergt C_____ who was also very groggy. It took us all night to get back here, with umpteen sit-downs, and we got into the barn at daylight.

Have been studying the view through the barn door for several days now. The R.A.M.C. staff keep coming in but don't seem able to mend me up. The M.O. has been in and says I shall have to go back to a Field Hospital for a week. Shall be alright then, so the Ambulance is calling here in a bit. It's the first time I shall not be with them; after all one does not like to be left out of it.

It is mid-day here at a clearing station, our Battalion Ambulance brought 6 of us down here this morning. Have been examined and passed on. They have just given us a meal here and we are waiting for the regular Ambulance convoy to go on to the Field Hospital wherever that is. There are quite a number of fellows here, from many different Regiments.

This is the Field Hospital at V_____ *[probably Vauchelles]*. Have not seen much of it, been on my back until today when am sitting up a bit. Had a very jolty ride down here in a 'tin lizzie' Red Cross car, 5 of us altogether.

"One of our sentry posts, working in pairs, they relieve each other from dusk till dawn, neither leaving the post. Hebuterne." "Sep. 22.15."

Was examined on arrival and 'put to bed', the 'bed' being a straw mattress on the floor of a large barn. There seem to be about 50 patients here, most of them are in the tents somewhere outside, the others are in this long barn. All the staff are R.A.M.C. men, no females. The food is the same as we have been having, but better cooked and served altho they can provide "dainties" when the case needs them. We are out of range here and are not bothered with shells. Seems funny not to hear one sometimes, the first few days out of range for what seems an age.

Had a most amazing experience today, was got on my feet for an hour, and after being a week on my back and seeing all things and people from the floor level I seemed to be about 8 or 9 feet tall. Could not get rid of it, everyone seemed puny and short; in fact ducked to pass under a cross beam which was 2 feet above my head. Walked up the barn and back clinging on to anything handy, was glad to get down again after 120 minutes. These are very long days, think I have read the last few letters from home about 50 times. There are a few old magazines but they are in great demand.

This place seems to take cases that are likely to get well again in a week or so, such as slight superficial wounds, bad colds and such like, or anything that need a few days rest. Quite a number of Regts are represented, but I have not seen anyone I know as yet. The fellows who can walk about from the tents outside come in and chat to us which breaks the monotony for a bit, for the inaction here is a terrific contrast, and to have nothing whatever to do, after being so full of everything, is a mental strain almost unexplainable.

FARM BUILDINGS AT
B—

"Artistic Weather Vanes, constructed in iron and copper, noticed in various villages: Bus-les-Artois (this was on our Dressing Station)." "Farm Buildings at B——. Sep. 14.15."

"Artistic Weather Vanes, constructed in iron and copper, noticed in various villages: Bus-les-Artois." "Barn at B_____. Sep. 14,15."

STABLE AT H.

SEP. 1. 15.

"Artistic Weather Vanes, constructed in iron and copper, noticed in various villages: Hebuterne." "Stable at H____. Sep. 1.15."

"Artistic Weather Vanes, constructed in iron and copper, noticed in various villages: Hebuterne." "House at H_____. Sep. 1.15." "The South mark is broken off this one and the G is west, the French for West being Guest."

Have been thoroughly examined and am to get up in the morning and have a walk outside with help, also had a Padre in, nice fellow and takes his job very sensibly. Does not punch religion down you wholesale but weaves it in around general topics and small talk. Quite enjoyed his company.

Arose as per schedule, and with assistance got to the bottom of the field and back. It's quite a little camp outside, very nicely situated with a wood nearby. I then sat at the door of the barn and watched an Irish Division march by. They are passing on their way up to the front, all complete with cookers, baggage wagons, Brass Hats and the rest of it. Fine lot of fellows, there is no mistake this affair is taking the cream of the country's manhood. Was fetched away for another exam by the M.O.-in-Chief. He was not long and ordered me back to my straw, and gathered that things are not exactly as I thought, but these people never tell you anything definite.

Must now go back a few days. The morning after my exam by the chief M.O., an orderly came and took my name, number, Regt, and told me to dress, as I had to go farther back, probably to Rouen. Great shock this, thought I was doing very well. However, it was not long before 4 of us were helped into an Ambulance Car. We were all 'sitting' cases so just one orderly accompanied us. Our pals of the past week waved goodbye to us as we turned into the roadway. What a bumpy ride, the roads have suffered from the enormous traffic they have to carry night and day. As we proceeded, other cars joined us, and before long counted 15 other Red Cross cars behind, and there were many in front as well. Truly a procession of pain winding its way to the rail-head, for that was our destination we found out, and also that this convoy runs every day from various Field Hospitals, and direct from the Front with bad cases. At mid-day we passed through a fairly large town (D___ *[unidentified],* I think) to the railway station yard. The preceding cars had commenced to unload their burdens, many stretcher cases among them. We were assisted from our 'bus' into a large shed, where we were put at a table and given a hot meal of stew and potatoes, jolly good and acceptable. There would be about 50 of us, all termed 'sitting cases'. After the meal we went outside the shed to where were sitting 6 Doctors, (Army Doctors of course) with a clerk each, so they took 6 of us fellows at a time. I got in front of a Scottie; had a job to follow his questions, but he was very nice and patient. His clerk wrote out an official card to keep in my pocket, also a large label, which he tied on my tunic, setting forth to whomsoever I should after come in contact, my name, number, Regt, religion, complaint, date, and other stuff. So thus labeled like parcels, we were taken to where a Red Cross train was standing with steam up, and what a train, tremendous length, corridor right through, end to end. After painful effort on the part of many we got settled 8 in a compartment. I got a window seat so could look out. What a sight! One does not take much notice of an odd sling or two, but to see slings and bandages by the hundred, well, it makes you think, and think, and think: heaps of stretchers, scores of heads and arms in bandages, and those with legs alright helping those with legs all wrong.

Eventually they were all got on board, and we moved out of the station. Directly after, a nurse came along the corridor with oranges and cigarettes, which she distributed amongst us. Also told us that we were going direct to Rouen, where there were many fully equipped Hospitals and we should get in about mid-night. Amongst the 8 of us, there was one with a bullet hole in his arm, another a bit of shell had gashed his head, a motor driver with a smashed wrist through a back-fire, another had an internal complaint – he seemed very poorly. In fact, the nurse took him away to lie down, (for the nurse kept visiting us). And so we sped on, relating experiences and

"Artistic Weather Vanes, constructed in iron and copper, noticed in various villages: Sailly-au-Bois." "Shop at S___ au B____."

"Artistic Weather Vanes, constructed in iron and copper,
noticed in various villages: Sailly-au-Bois — I think the
house was used as a chapel." "House at S___ au B_____."

"Artistic Weather Vanes, constructed in iron and copper, noticed in various villages: Sailley-au-Bois" "Private House at S___ au B_____." "Sept. 4. – These are weather vanes, they appear to be cut from sheet iron & some of the designs are very curious, but only on a few can be seen the compass points N.S.E.W. You see only one in this four. I may get you a few more of these as we have more about."

"Artistic Weather Vanes, constructed in iron and copper,
noticed in various villages: A Restaurant (cafe) Courcelles."
"Shop at C____."

watching the changing panorama through the windows until it got dark, then an orderly brought coffee in tin mugs and bread, butter and biscuits. Composing ourselves for a nap, we went on till just turned mid-night when the long train pulled into Rouen station.

Scores of R.A.M.C. people were waiting for us, and I lost my train companions and got to a double deck motor-bus. The inside was full, so struggled up the steps to the top, but being up above got a glimpse of the city for it was not so very dark. In half-an-hour the bus pulled into the yard of what we found after was a large convent. After being unloaded and our labels examined, me and a Sergt were detailed to a ward consisting of a long wood hut built with others in the yard. The orderly of this ward took us into a room therein, where we found a sponge bath with hot water. He gave us clean shirts and pyjamas and left us. The Sergt had a smashed shoulder, so I washed him and myself. The orderly had been seeing to others, but came back when we were ready and took us into the ward. We stood at the door and took in the scene with hungry and glaring eyes: electric lights with red shades, the night nurse in spotless white, two long rows of beds — ACTUAL BEDS with clean sheets, most of them occupied with clean-shaven men, cleanliness everywhere, and the dim soft red light over all. Goodness!! Heaven on earth... He shewed us our beds; I got in and lay on my back and breathed long and deep, exquisite was the feel of clean linen.

Was told this morning that I should have to stay in bed a day or two, so water, towel and soap was brought by the orderly. (There appears to be one orderly and two nurses in this hut of 24 beds). Breakfast arrived after in a kind of entrée dish, one for each of us, also an enamel mug into which coffee was poured from a large jug. During the morning the contents of my pockets were brought to me and my label tied on the bed-head together

Flowers from Flanders fields – poppies and cornflowers. Our table? decorations. July 1915.

with my chart, then followed an exam by the M.O., but gathered nothing from him. Introduced myself to my next bed mate, also a Corporal, badly dished up in the hand, arm and shoulder with shrapnel. Dinner arrived in the entrée dish again, good food, well cooked. There are many books and magazines here, so have got hold of a 'Marie Corelli'.

The M.O. passed me this morning but understand from the nurse that some special stuff is going to be put on my leg some time today; the orderly says he won't half slap it on too! Comic chap, he is, comes from Dublin, tries to keep us all merry and bright as far as possible.

Got the stuff put on yesterday and am now in a sort of straitjacket one side. Can just manage to sit up for meals. Shall be like this for several days, so shall have to leave this as the nurse will not let me sit up only just for meals.

Had my leg freed this morning after 5 days, have just a couple of bandages on now. Do not know the result, but can sit up and take notice. This last few days have been long, altho most certainly am getting a good rest. There is a nice fellow who chats to me, Jock, a Scottie; has a wound in his shoulder but is about every day, helps with meals and other odd jobs about the ward. Expects to be well in about a week, then will have to go to a training camp just outside the town for a fortnight, then back to his Regt.

The orderly brought a gramophone in today, had a few records going, but not many, for have to think of the other chaps. One poor fellow in the top bed is in a very bad way, shrapnel all over him and had many operations. He moans badly sometimes. Understand this is rather a big Hospital converted from a Convent; several huts like this are built in the yard and grounds. The M.O. has been since dinner and I am to get onto my feet in the morning and potter about the ward a bit to see what happens. Fancy he must be a bit puzzled over my leg?

Been up four hours today, and got about very well. Been rolling bandages, writing letters for a couple of fellows with bad arms. Had a chat with the Sergt who came in with me, he is going well.

The days are very similar now, am still pottering about with a crutch, the poor fellow in the top bed passed out this morning. His bed was screened round, and we all saluted as he was carried out covered with a Union Jack. R.I.P.

Have to stay in bed in the morning for another exam. The orderly tells me there is a boat leaving for England in a couple of days, and there is always an exam to see who has to go on it.

Three doctors were on the examination tour this morning. They all had a go at me, but did not say anything to me, but only consulted among themselves. The boat list will be posted up in the ward tonight.

My name figured on the list last night, so presume I shall be leaving for Blighty on Wednesday; suppose they have done all they can here.

Expect this is the last bit I shall write in this country for a bit anyway; am ready for the Ambulance which leaves for the docks at 12. Am now in uniform again, duly labeled etc. Had a job with boots, it appears an unwritten law to send people to England in the worst boots available, leaving the better ones for those going back up the line, and quite right too.

TYPES. Some

The Parson.

The "Doc" (M.O

WRITINGS AND DRAWINGS FROM THE TRENCHES

"Drawn during a weeks stay in 3rd R.A.M.C. Field Hospital at Vouchelles." "TYPES. Somewhere in France? — The Parson. — The "Doc" (M.O.) — "Jock".

151

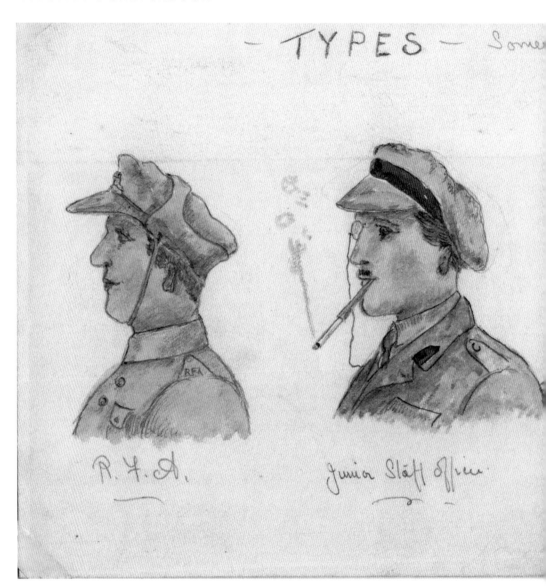

- TYPES - Some

R. F. A.

Junior Staff Officer.

in France?

moto Cyclist-

Oct 14.15.

"Drawn during a weeks stay in
3rd R.A.M.C. Field Hospital at
Vouchelles." "TYPES. Somewhere in
France? — R.F.A. — Junior Staff
Officer — Motor Cyclist — Oct. 14.15."

Memory Sketch of "A" Hut Rouen Nov. 15

"a memory of "a" Hut ho. 3
Stationery Hospital. Rouen, France."
"Memory Sketch of "a" hut, Rouen.
Nov. 1915."

Second Southern Queen
Victoria Auxiliary Hospital.
Bristol. 1455

Soldiers in hospital blues. Second Southern Queen Victoria
Auxiliary Hospital. Bristol. c.1915–1918. (Henry spent some
time being treated here)

We are now lying off Southampton, it's a brilliant sunny morning. We had a splendid trip down the river, but when we got outside Havre and dropped the pilot she began to roll somewhat, so I spent the rest of the crossing on my back. Am alright this morning and enjoying the sunshine. All we sitting cases are left very much to ourselves; the attention of the staff is rightly concentrated on the stretcher cases. We are now moving into the dock and can see a train evidently waiting for us with a lot of St John's Ambulance men.

This is in the train, but no-one knows where we are going. It's not a corridor train, so there's 8 of us on our own with a packet of sandwiches each. We are going north-wards and that's all we know.

I am in bed at Cheltenham, a school converted into a Hospital. It is a civillian affair, the local doctors (all praise to them) doing the work. Have been examined again and having fresh treatment entirely. A long piece of wood from waist to heel, all bound up to keep me rigid in bed for a week past, but managed to write home and let them know where and how I am.

Getting about now with crutches, been for a motor ride through the kindness of a lady who visits here. It's getting on for Christmas now, and am hoping to be home by then.

This is Christmas day, have just eaten my Christmas dinner with the wife and kiddie, for which we are all very thankful. But have remembered those who are still out there, especially the old pals who are in little plots of ground that will be England for ever, and that this upheaval will speedily end, and the others will be restored to their homes and people.

I present
– in the pink.

Christmas card. 48th Division, 1916. This
Christmas card was sent home by soldiers
serving with 48th Division, which included 1/5th
Gloucesters. It is quite possible that Henry Buckle
received one or more of these from chums still
at the front.

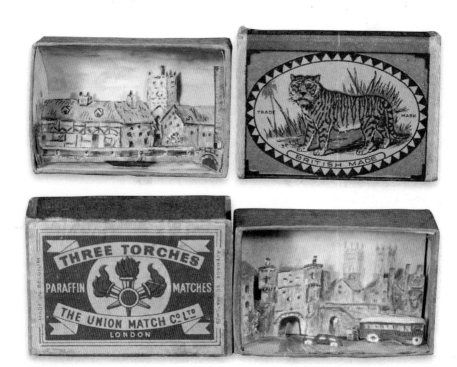

Tewkesbury Abbey and York Minster. These two cut-out paper models in matchboxes were made by Henry Buckle in the 1930s, judging by the styles of the bus and car. From Gloucestershire to Yorkshire, via the Western Front.